HURRICANE
IN A
BAD MOOD

HURRICANE IN A BAD MOOD

poems by
SUE OWEN

University of Louisiana at Lafayette Press
2024

http://ulpress.org
University of Louisiana at Lafayette Press
P.O. Box 43558
Lafayette, LA 70504-3558

Library of Congress Cataloging-in-Publication Data

Names: Owen, Sue, 1942- author.
Title: Hurricane in a bad mood / Sue Owen.
Other titles: Hurricane in a bad mood (Compilation)
Description: Lafayette, LA : University of Louisiana at Lafayette
Press, 2024.
Identifiers: LCCN 2024033898 | ISBN 9781959569176 (paperback)
Subjects: LCGFT: Poetry.
Classification: LCC PS3565.W564 H87 2024 | DDC 811/.54--
dc23/eng/20240724
LC record available at https://lccn.loc.gov/2024033898

PRAISE FOR SUE OWEN'S BOOKS

Nursery Rhymes for the Dead

"*Nursery Rhymes for the Dead* approaches and questions earth's fear and danger. It does this with formal simplicity and the choice of generic words, words without trademarks to muffle or mislead. These are poems of pressures that exist outside the pressures of our time. New to Sue Owen's work, I find here a first book that is consistent and graceful. It suggests maturity and deserves respect."

—Laura Jensen

"Sue Owen has an active Gothic imagination and a fine control of her material. I enjoyed reading this book."

—Margaret Atwood

The Book of Winter

"Reading this book is like walking along with an immensely gifted companion who is playful and communicative: everything encountered on the walk is enticed into displaying its talents and inner feelings. You even begin to acquire the gift yourself, and you feel that no walk will ever be *pedestrian* again! Whatever is touched in this book pours out its hidden feelings, its history, its significance for you and your life."

—William Stafford

"There is a fine logic of fantasy in these poems, a kind of ruthless grammar of supposition that is startling in itself and happily accompanied by a direct plainness of language, rapid and unsparing."

—W. S. Merwin

"Sue Owen has what Wallace Stevens called a 'mind of winter' and, consequently, she finds snow in her name and ice in her imagination, a chilling blankness at the heart of things. She is a poet of zero sums and mathematical clarities, a witty parabolist of the void. *The Book of Winter* beautifully and unflinchingly evokes what Stevens identified as 'nothing that is not there and the nothing that is.'"

—Edward Hirsch

My Doomsday Sampler

"Experiencing Sue Owen's poems explains why poetry is considered the Queen of the Arts; each poem is a curve toward the quiet space you've been saving your life to live in. The dainty filigree in the quality of her thought is fused to an unblinking intensity, and if her vision of the world is freighted with dark, allegorical pointings, the poems remain obstinately accessible in a double sense. You know the meaning of every word, and those words mean to make you accessible to yourself."

—Jack Myers

"There is something very special about Sue Owen's work. These poems are all in one voice, indeed one tone of voice—a well-wrought, well-worked-out development of poetic 'ideas.' She sets up a poem, usually presented in free-verse quatrains, like a proposition or an equation, then deftly, delicately, and elegantly works out the equation. Owen is a very sophisticated and innovative poet who has earned her reputation for excellence in the literary world."

—George Garrett

The Devil's Cookbook

"There is far more than lively wit at work in these brooding, obsessive poems. Sue Owen has a gift for symbol and allegory, and she has undertaken no less than a review of Dante's (or Milton's, or anyone's) Hell. There are so many masterful poems in this collection one hardly knows where to begin to cite them."

—Daniel Mark Epstein

"Sue Owen's proclivity for bleak comedy takes shapely form here in a series of quirky quatrains aimed at what she playfully depicts as the devil in the flesh of everything. A poetic sharp-shooter, she hits one malign target after another!"

—Sandra M. Gilbert

"In this fourth collection, *The Devil's Cookbook*, Sue Owen ponders vast unanswerable questions with a remarkable facility and ease. Owen's sensibility is original and full of surprises. Like stars, these dark unflinching poems throw off all kinds of metaphysical sparks."

—Elizabeth Spires

ACKNOWLEDGMENTS

*My thanks again to Thomas Owen, my family,
and especially to all my friends.*

Poems in this collection have appeared in the following magazines and anthologies:

The Atlanta Review, "A Tempest in the Teapot"; *The Connecticut Review*, "Why the Fern Uncurls"; *5 A.M.*, "Think About the Coffin"; *Louisiana Literature*, "Another House Plant," "Flying Off the Handle," "Hurricane and Its Eye," "Last Nail in the Coffin," "Tell About the Trees," and "When the Roof is Gone"; *The Louisiana Review*, "Top Kill Fails" and "What the Mold Likes"; *The New Delta Review*, "Solitude" and "Water Everywhere"; *Ploughshares*, "A House Sparrow" and "Shot in the Foot"; *Salmagundi*, "Instructions for the Nail"; *The Southwest Review*, "Even the Dead Do It" and "Hit the Nail on the Head"; *The Good Grief Journal*, "Even the Dead Do It"; *The Southern Poetry Anthology: Louisiana*, "Hurricane and Its Eye" and "Tell About the Trees"; and *Verse Daily*, "Even the Dead Do It."

"Why the Fern Uncurls" was the winner of the Gretchen Warren Award for the best poem published in the previous year by a member of the New England Poetry Club.

TABLE OF CONTENTS

I

This is the Last Straw 3
Think of the Coffin 4
The Doomed Snowflake 5
A House Sparrow......................................6
The Riddle of Dirty Hands.......................7
Instructions for the Nail 8
Hurricane in a Bad Mood 9
Where the Dead Go 10

II

A Roll of the Dice 13
Last Nail in the Coffin............................14
Nailed to the Truth 15
Hurricane Worries a Lot.........................16
More Than Housework 17
When Pelicans Cannot Fly......................18
In the Window Box 19
And is Such a Small Word 20
What the Mold Likes 21
Even the Dead Do It..............................22

III

The Death Wish......................................25
Why the Fern Uncurls............................26
My Song for the Night...........................27
The Story of Frostbite 28
Mountain Out of a Molehill...................29
Another House Plant 30
That Common Comma...........................31
Water Everywhere..................................32
A Poem About True Grime 33
Hit the Nail on the Head........................34

IV

Why the Snow Falls 37
Solitude 38
Hurricane and its Eye 39
Flying Off the Handle...............................40
Tell About the Trees 41
When the Roof is Gone 42
Here is the Watering Can 43
Asterisk Tries to Explain 44
Top Kill Fails 45
Learning the Hard Way.............................46
More About the Grave Diggers................47

V

Just Pieces in a Puzzle.............................51
A Tempest in the Teapot 52
No One Likes Rot......................................53
These are the Pitfalls................................54
The Gulf Turns into Tears.........................55
Shot in the Foot 56
Heart in the Right Place 57
If the Dead Could Dream.........................58
Hurricane Gone Crazy..............................59
Star Watch 60
Nailed in for Good....................................61

"And the darkness there,
think of it as a new universe,
but without stars to wish on."

I

THIS IS THE LAST STRAW

The last straw that broke
that poor camel's back
didn't know it was so heavy.
It thought it was just

as light and thin as sunlight,
just one of many straws
that blows in a brisk wind.
It thought it was just as

insignificant as any grain
there in that meadow,
one that might become bedding
for dreams to sleep on,

or packing that would protect.
How could the last straw
know what harsh fate had
in mind for it, that fate

was not just clutching
at any ordinary straw on
that day while that camel
waited, patient and strong?

Who would have thought
that camel's mute backbone
was slowly measuring weight,
the way that time carries its

minutes forward toward an end?
What could have stopped
the last straw in time?
Which warning would cry out?

THINK OF THE COFFIN

Think of the wood coffin
as just a box for putting
favored objects away, but
this time not the stray buttons.

No, not old shoes either.
More like someone's bones,
and they will be yours,
packed tightly into that space.

And the darkness there,
think of it as a new universe,
but without stars to wish on.
In fact, there won't be

the slightest bit of light
after the lid is nailed shut,
after the first shovelfuls
of dirt throw down their weight.

So think about how in there
you will be all alone
in that grim graveyard,
buried out of sight and time,

so to speak, hidden away
and forgotten by the living,
except for the one stone above
that remembers your name,

if the wind and rain don't
wear its memory down. If
they do, think what it
is like to be forgotten forever.

THE DOOMED SNOWFLAKE

Delicate as an eyelash,
it blinks in the wind as
it spins and tumbles downward
on its blind journey, one

of the many doomed to fall.
Fragile as thin glass,
it twinkles for a second,
one of the many jewels

of winter worn on a twisted
branch before it is doomed
to melt, temporary as breath.
Perhaps the beauty of ice

and crystal is just that,
how brittle its geometry is,
its lace also intricate
and weak and vulnerable,

one of the many easily
crushed and doomed to break.
It is so light and ethereal
and frail that any weight,

like a foot or a shovel,
or a boot that stomped it,
could turn it into slush.
So neither the poor snowflake

nor you can be protected
from those forces of doom,
the harsh realities of time
that tick to destroy us.

A HOUSE SPARROW

Sometimes I've wondered why
it seems happy enough.
It hangs around like a meek
reminder of smallness,

and chirps its slight sound,
and flashes its dull brown,
in the vague green of summer.
And it must think that

there in the spread of leaf,
where it pauses on a branch,
it is hardly ever noticed,
which is almost true.

But today as I stare at it
and think of all things small,
the dust, flies, and stars,
the house sparrow's hopping

seems to matter as one
small detail that is always
there to prove a larger point,
one addition to the day.

And it must like to belong
there with the wind and sun.
It must somehow know
it is important and that

itself must make it glad
to go on and sing for us,
against the sky, that one
repeated syllable of its note.

THE RIDDLE OF DIRTY HANDS

Why is it that our hands
are always getting dirty
from whatever they touch,
like tools and silverware,

railings, chairs, or books?
And whatever they touch,
whether it seems to be
as clear as a mirror or

as bright as a window, why
is there that thick layer
of dirt that waits for
them, or the thick layer,

on the shoes and the floor,
of that outright grime?
Doesn't it almost seem
that the dirt is somehow

necessary as it collects
on knobs and letters,
as it works itself into our
clothes and even into brooms?

Tell me why our hands
can never stop that desire
of dirt to come closer and
to soil them every day.

How does it really help
when our hands keep washing
themselves clean with all that
pure water and soap?

INSTRUCTIONS FOR THE NAIL

So what, that you were
born to be too sharp for
your own good, and your future
to come would only lead

to your being nailed in.
So what, that you thought
the hammer wouldn't notice you,
and some hand wouldn't

choose you to be the one.
You had it coming to you
the minute you became a nail,
all the usual problems

about force and submission,
all of that about destiny,
how the stars had planned it,
maybe something, too, about

the inexplicable mutterings
of the steel you are or fate.
So these are the instructions
you never wanted to hear.

These are the guidelines
that tell you how to accept you
are a nail and always will be.
There are hard times ahead

for you, the confusion about
the past and the crossroads
where you will have no choice,
not even the chance to say no.

HURRICANE IN A BAD MOOD

Why did you just hate me
as my wild winds howled
your ridiculous roofs off
and knocked your cheap

windows in and shook
your timbers so hard that
you thought you would die?
Wasn't my speed what you

waited for, my strength
what you knew would come?
Weren't my days of rain
the lessons you had to learn,

as the mirrors in your
rooms flooded or drowned
your future so that if
you had any plans left

you would abandon them
before my mold crept in?
Didn't you know that
your houses and your lives

were fragile and that I
could twirl them with
the bold truth of my clouds,
darker than trouble in

a hurry to teach you all
the pain and suffering you
would never escape, so
each of you would become mine?

WHERE THE DEAD GO

They go down, not up,
down the way leaves fall
and turn crisp in the autumn,
down the way snow falls

and covers the grim landscape,
down, down their bones go
buried in their coffins,
down into the earth where

the darkness covers them up,
down into the cold oblivion
of the past and forgetting,
too far from the living,

so far down there is nothing
left in their memories to
see and no reason to hear
when they lie that deep,

down, down, down in graves
beyond pain and wanting,
beyond the hand of time
that makes the sun and stars

repeat their motions and
the seasons follow by rote,
down into the blind universe
of the roots, the worms,

and the indifferent stones,
down beneath the headstone,
where the changes to the body
begin, down, down, down, down.

II

A ROLL OF THE DICE

Why should those two
care who throws them,
or where, or how they fall?
They are just dark dots

someone carved into bone.
They are already numb to
the numbers they represent,
and any combination

from two to twelve never
changes their shape or fate.
So what if money or
wishes are bet on them?

It's almost a waste of time,
as those two are rattled
and then thrown down hard.
It doesn't even matter

to them if luck or bad
luck breathes, or spits on
them, or gives them a kiss.
It all adds up the same

to them whether they turn
up in this game like snake
eyes that stare or double
boxcars that only blink.

Their apathy knows that
chance made up its mind a
long time ago, when each star
took its assigned place.

LAST NAIL IN THE COFFIN

Not just one of many,
it's odd now that I was chosen
as the last nail driven
into this box of a coffin,

to become, with the force
of the hammer, the decisive
one who will name the end,
the last definition of death.

And it's odd to know that
because I am so sharp and
direct nothing more needs
to be said about the conclusion

afterwards, not a word from
the brute hammer that never
had a conscience, not even
a groan from this mute coffin

as it took the pounding.
Even this body that I hold
tightly inside the shut
lid will remain always speechless

and listening for nothing,
because with my sharpest
tongue I pronounced the last.
And though I could hold

together a house for a life,
it's my odd job here as
the last nail in to hold forever
this dark forgetting beneath.

NAILED TO THE TRUTH

Now the nail dreams of
flying through the wood.
In that dream it sees
the grains of wood up close,

like waves of time it breaks
through to reach infinity.
There it hears the rings of
the tree that grow and sing,

as the rainwater rises up
to bless the leaves' future.
There it sees the memory
of daylight rinse the twigs

with promise and the branches
with the pain waiting in hope.
And, in so deep, and almost
unaware of its sharpness,

the nail doesn't ever want
that flying dream to stop,
though it hears the hammer
pound it like a distant shout

that tells it to wake up.
Then the hammer calls to it
with the rhythm of anger,
and with that loud truth

that tells the nail its
flying dream is now over.
Then the nail buried deep in
the wood forever knows this.

HURRICANE WORRIES A LOT

How did I know that their
bayous and low swamps,
their live oaks, pecky
cypresses, and brown pelicans

couldn't take the force
that my winds packed?
Hadn't they been warned
about my temper and punch?

Didn't they see my might
coming, the predictions
that the time had come?
Whose fault is it then,

when they try to blame me
for all their heart-wrenching
stories about what they lost?
Why do they only point

the finger of blame at me
for their furniture lost, keys,
mementos, pictures lost,
even those piles of the dead

that turned up drowned?
How could all this disaster
be my doing, all this pain
and loss left on my hands,

unless I have become what
is the greatest evil ever, my
winds so out of control that
I make perfection look easy?

MORE THAN HOUSEWORK

Here is the water, the pail,
and brush that know how to
speak all the right words
that make the floor

want to be clean again.
It doesn't matter how much
dirt the shoes brought in
or if the dirt was caked mud.

It doesn't matter how much
dust has swirled in through
the window or under the door,
or if the dust has gathered

under the bed and in corners.
There always was a good
way to talk back to dirt,
and, especially, soap knows

this language that cleans
with its bubble and foam.
And the broom, too, knows
the language of the sweep,

and the dust mop knows
the language of how to
collect and shake dust out.
So there is no place, really,

where dirt can hide, no word
that won't be spoken to it.
This is why dirt must listen
hard and always obey it.

WHEN PELICANS CANNOT FLY

Yes, they were born brown,
but that doesn't mean
they like to bathe in oil.
That doesn't mean they like

to nest near the toxic brew,
or like to smell its stink.
Oil doesn't mix well with
water, and neither does it

suit the brown pelicans,
who must eat their fish
basted in oil and swallow
the whole mess in one gulp.

What must the pelicans
be thinking of us now,
when they cannot fly, must
perch alone on their islands,

their heads hunched back
on their shoulders, their
pouches tucked in, their
long bills at rest on

their chests, because they
cannot fly, swim, or eat, so
they eye us and their death?
And when their feathers

have turned this brown
from the oil and their soaked
wings can no longer glide,
who can answer that stare?

IN THE WINDOW BOX

Those white geraniums that
you planted there look
curious as they now lift
the necks of their long

stems, so they can better
see the morning sun.
And their flowers must bloom
there because they like

what they see, such radiance
and dazzle that they want
to talk back, as if each
new blossom there is a word

spoken to that window light.
And the watering you do
each day, and the growing
that goes on, so this

conversation can continue,
must cause the green leaves
to spread their own chatter.
Even though other plants

prefer to live in silent
worship of the sun, you
know that those white geraniums'
talking must be going on

because each of their blossoms
looks like a large head
with purposeful ideas
taking seed in those brains.

AND IS SUCH A SMALL WORD

AND is such a small word
for all it does to
connect and hold together.
AND it takes a lot of

strength for AND to do
this with just three letters,
not at all like TO or IT,
which have their own problems

with their size and tasks.
Take, for example, THE, which
only introduces, or BUT,
which is always interfering,

or NOW, which just announces.
AND's work is harder because,
besides that it is small,
it has to be as mighty

as glue or even the nail.
There is no comparison to
YET, which changes its mind,
or WHY, which asks too many

questions, or NOT, which
is way too negative.
No, AND knows its place
between, and how never to

receive much attention,
and never to think about
how disconnected this world
would be without it.

WHAT THE MOLD LIKES

It goes without saying
that the mold likes water,
or even better, flooding, so
it can stay around awhile

and infect a whole house
with its slime and stink
on the walls, creeping up
them and over the furniture

like a shadow let loose.
Then it likes to linger there,
with that first hint of death,
so it can damage even paper,

fabric, and wood with its
darkest reasons for rot,
and leave them all soft
and soggy like doomed leaves

at the bottom of a swamp.
Also, the mold likes the
warmest air that helps its
thought process and stirs up

its plans like a slow brew, so
nothing in the house is
worth saving, so each surface
it has touched becomes

corrupted by this change
that is worse than destruction
to be dreaded and is harder
to get rid of than fear.

EVEN THE DEAD DO IT

Feel regret about the one
event that led them there,
the cough that cracked the rib,
the ladder rung that broke

the neck, or the knife that
plunged too deep into the heart.
It's all a matter of perspective,
the dead think, as they lie

in that underground darkness.
It's all a matter of the silence
of eternity, as no breath
ever comes back for a short

visit, even for old times' sake.
And since the dead can't talk,
what else is there to do
but to think hard about the pain

and brevity of their lives,
the lost chances and wrong turns?
But even that could lead
to many headaches and the old

insomnia, when death was
billed as peaceful, even serene.
So why trouble with the thinking,
after all, the dead think?

All that is required of us in
this cemetery is what our bones
politely arranged, what the
prayer meant as the coffin shut.

III

THE DEATH WISH

I'm not that first star
in the fading blue,
just peeking over the horizon,
that you might wish on.

No, I'm not that simple.
Stars don't make me come true.
Nor am I that good-luck
penny shining beneath your

foot like a little false moon.
No, I'm never the one that
specializes in bringing you
a season of flickering light,

and am not that one candle
on your cake burning with
another year ahead for you.
Neither would I ever be

the good luck that you want
waiting in that wishbone,
nor in your crossed fingers,
nor in that salt you

might throw over your shoulder.
All of the other superstitions
that could bring you hope
are not what death promises,

for I am the only wish
that thrives on your pain
and your dark despair, the one
wish that snuffs you out.

WHY THE FERN UNCURLS

It isn't guesswork why
the fern uncurls its fronds
like a hand whose fist
gradually opens with each

finger, one at a time, or it
uncurls like a knot whose
threads fall loose suddenly,
or like secrets that slide

out, too soon, on a tongue.
The fern knows this is true.
To uncurl is to reveal,
at last, with those gestures

the unknown as it gives up
its life in the shadows,
gives up its own silence
and its dreams in the dark.

Then all the fern knows is
forgiven and it can't turn
back, so it releases its
green gladly into the sun

in its future and grows
as it was told to do.
Nothing else is certain to
the fern but that uncurling

and that growing, as time
has finally touched it.
Nothing else matters but for
the fern to forget its past.

MY SONG FOR THE NIGHT

Let someone else write
the common song for the day
and its pretty sunlight
that sparkles all over.

I'm the one who will write
the song for the night,
its mystery and shadows.
I'm the one who will fill

in all the dark notes that
will carry the melody
for the stars, and sleep,
and even for the dreams,

over the locked houses.
It will be a beautiful song
rising above into the dark
corners of the universe.

It will be full of its own
dark daring, not a lament,
but with a slow beat.
And those dark words will

reveal all the secrets
and fears that live there,
so that the song will
always remain like a memory.

I'm the one who will write
the song for the night,
carried by my breath into
the darkness that is endless.

THE STORY OF FROSTBITE

They say I am frostbite,
but I used no teeth
when I nipped those toes.
And I wasn't even hungry

when those fingers turned blue.
They also say I tried to
take someone's life, that
those shivers were from

my touch, that chill from
my cold breath and heart.
They even say that I have
the coldest blood, actually

ice running in my veins,
so that when I bleed,
I drip like a sharp icicle.
They don't ever admire my

frostwork on those windows,
when I am just peeking in.
They don't see my beauty
at all well enough, though

the snowflake gets attention
for its intricate crystal,
and its snow that falls
with a purity that seems

to cleanse their landscape.
No, it's always my fault
when death steps in or pain.
My other name is blame.

MOUNTAIN OUT OF A MOLEHILL

It's not easy making
a mountain out of a puny
molehill, thinks that mole.
It requires a great deal

of dirt, more than the mole
can find or shovel, with
its pathetic, little paws.
It requires much determination

and a passion for size
that the mole doubts it has.
It requires an obsession
with all of the details for

this undertaking, all of
the trivia looming in
the mole's dreams to puff
them up, to make hope grand,

to make height important,
but the mole prefers its
humble darkness in the earth
to the vanity of clouds.

Still, there is a chance that
the mole will actually work
itself up into the correct
frenzy and carry it out,

turn that molehill from
just a simple activity
and just a few words into
one large mountain of thought.

ANOTHER HOUSE PLANT

These shy violets only
want a little light or
even just a dim windowsill,
because they are subdued

and don't ever expect much.
Besides preferring darkness,
they don't even need
much water either, as if

only a little attention is
what they thrive on best
to produce their small bursts
of that one emotion

that we call their flowers.
And when that first purple
does arrive, carefully
opening above their flat

and soft leaves, the spectacle
of these violets blooming
is always as quiet as
any news spread by only

the hint of a whisper,
so that no statement is
made, no declaration other
than purple's own purpose

as it sends out its glow,
not to the day, but to all
who understand that power
in their unrestrained will.

THAT COMMON COMMA

So ordinary on the page,
a little footprint between
the words to say our breath
stopped here to sit under

a tree and perhaps daydream,
or to listen to the verbs
that sing their birdsongs
about the flight of the mind.

Then our breath has no
concern while it rests here,
pausing on this little rock,
as sure as a solid noun

in a landscape of adjectives,
helping out the grasses or
clouds to pick their details.
And yet that common comma,

poised between the clauses,
knows it must let us and
the sentence go on down
that troubled road to the end

of the idea that started it.
So we will move on through
these words, or wait again,
elsewhere, to obey it and

to take one breath at a time.
Isn't that what that common
comma has been teaching us?
How to measure our lives?

WATER EVERYWHERE

Too much heavy rain when
this rain came and then too
many drops of rain,
like the tears that came

after the long pain of too
many days of this rain.
Too many flooded streets
to make the pain worse.

Too many flooded houses.
Too many rooms in which
the water kept rising
up over chairs, tables, beds,

and dreams, in fact, too
much water that seeped
in, so that every minute
and hour became soggy,

bogged down by the weight
of too much of this rain.
Too many cloudy days in
a row and too many trees

dripping, too many birds
so wet they didn't dare fly.
Too much rain on the roof
with its relentless pounding.

Too much persistence by
this water as it increased
the leaking and flooding.
Too much damage to the soul.

A POEM ABOUT TRUE GRIME

It's not just any dirt here,
what the shoes brought
in and is relatively fresh.
It isn't the light dust

that just settled down
to coat the room with it.
Nor is it the dust that
piles up in the corners or

is quite out of reach.
That dust, which is also
unwanted, can easily
be swished or swept away.

I'm talking about true
grime, such as that which
rings the bathroom tub,
toilet bowl, and the sink

with its reckless slime,
or like a curse made by
the devil that is so strong
it seems nothing can

remove its shadow or stain.
Nothing can remove that
filth either from the kitchen
sink or where it cakes up

on the stove or in the oven.
This, then, is the mission
of true grime to make us
all the slaves to its power.

HIT THE NAIL ON THE HEAD

Yes, it's a head there
right on the top of that nail
and it does the thinking.
It thinks about the blow

that will come in its future,
and it dreams about the sound
of that awful pounding
in its worst nightmares.

And awake, it thinks, too,
about the hammer that
soon will come out of nowhere
to hit it, so that the two

of them are head-to-head
with a force that destroys
all the serious thinking,
maybe even destroys the head,

as the nail is driven deep.
Then all the thinking stops.
Then all that the head knows
is pain in a language

that only its body feels,
surrounded as it is by
the pressure of too much wood.
Then what was the reason

for the head of the nail
thinking all the time anyway?
How could any thought
have ever changed its fate?

IV

WHY THE SNOW FALLS

I can't really say for
sure, but it seems the snow
here falls as if it wants
to whisper its white to

the brown and dead earth
and to turn its words into
a promise, but what promise
I still can't yet say.

It also seems to whisper
the way that the last breath
does when it wants to stay
close to the body after

it has been asked to leave,
and the quiet way, too,
that its spirit always seems
to hover somewhere nearby.

And there is little I can
say about why the snow
here seems to take such care
to cover the bare branches

and why it seems to want
to bury the cold earth
under this peace and purity
with such a slow gesture.

But I do know that the snow
has turned itself, with
this falling, into something
much like a fresh grave.

SOLITUDE

Don't mention the aloof
clouds detached and isolated.
It's their own business if
they want to be distant.

That goes for the stars, too,
sparkling yet alone in
their vast space and darkness.
They probably like the silence.

As for the leaves' preference,
it's true they cluster, but
they, too, end up scattered
by the wind, become brittle

in unknown gutters or
random streets, as if they
don't mind the seclusion.
And it's apparent any stone

pretty much keeps to itself,
so cold and heavy there,
with just the dirt beneath it,
or perhaps a solitary coffin.

Especially the dead, too, may
like their remote positions,
certainly buried and out of
the way of the usual racket,

so there is nothing to bother
that depth of their solitude,
what some may call a peace,
at last the end of small talk.

HURRICANE AND ITS EYE

They say I'm calm here
at this center where my winds
don't blow and my sight
down to the earth stays clear.

They say my thoughts should
turn philosophical now as I
think over the devastation
I have brought: houses gone,

trees uprooted, shores
ragged and lacking definition.
And that now is the time
for me to see the advantage

of order over the chaos I prefer,
to think about the harm
of my reckless speed, the
wayward path of my strength.

They say this insight here
will lead to regret so that
I won't punish the living
anymore and won't try to

rearrange what was fixed.
I'm to call off the trouble
still building in my dark clouds,
as if I could reason with

my angry and turbulent winds,
but I say I can't collect
my wild thoughts or tame
the outer terror that claims me.

FLYING OFF THE HANDLE

Say you ended up in that
kitchen and you started to
fly off that proverbial handle,
I'd warn you about that.

I'd say you were so angry
you were losing your
grip on reason again, you
were skidding off reason's

edge, or just sinking into
the kingdom of the mad.
I'd be quite frank about it
and would warn you, as before,

that the cooking pan has
a handle for a good reason,
so no one is ever burned,
though the flame beneath it

has a tongue just for licking.
And fire, given the chance,
would be practicing when
it turned up the stove's heat.

So I'd warn you to be careful
of what sizzles or boils
and to use your potholder,
whatever that is to this

metaphorical scene, in which
handles convey the reason
for safety and care, including
the truth about hurt.

TELL ABOUT THE TREES

downed in a big wind,
their branches that crack
loose in pain and their
frightened leaves that shudder.

Or is it that their leaves
gasp as they twirl, or
is it that they scream?
Then that crash is the same,

isn't it, whether the trees
hit the ground and make
the dust jump, or whether
they smash the roof and

old tiles fly away from
what they were to protect?
Then the roots, you say,
tell about the roots,

twisted and up in the air,
practicing their own deadly
dance, and tell about
the trunks, then broken or

split because their weight
punishes them, and the gravity
that destroys their balance.
Tell about what's left

under those trees, you keep
on saying, tell what chance
there is for survival when
trees become the angels of ruin.

WHEN THE ROOF IS GONE

Perhaps, roofs are just
an idea constructed over
the head to keep out
the wind, rain, and cold.

Or perhaps, they are real
timbers and tiles and nails,
but it doesn't seem so,
when the wind blows them off.

Then the protection, or
the idea of it, is gone,
and the bare bones of
the house and the life there

become raw and exposed,
wind blowing what is precious
away and the rain chasing it.
So the idea that represents

safety and security
cannot hold, the idea of
ceiling, walls, and windows
disappears, too, and the idea

of closets and beds is gone,
leaving the past, or only
just the idea of it, since
the future isn't as safe as

it seems either, or breath.
Then there is nothing much
left to believe in, nothing
real, no permanence in hope.

HERE IS THE WATERING CAN

All these house plants
can do now is to wait for
that sprinkle of water as
they bask on the windowsill

in bright sun and keep on
with their growing, more
buds and leaves, maybe
a few more flowers for

amusement to pass the hours.
All they can do is hope
they won't dry out before
their new leaves turn yellow

and then wilt, or won't
just completely die, if
the water doesn't save them.
So their passive wishing

is all these house plants
have going for them, as if
it were a kind of prayer,
spoken to the house gods,

that may never be heard.
Or maybe the watering can
hears it when it also
waits nearby, knowing that

its purpose, as well as
water's, will help out right
now, just as every answer
always quenches each thirst.

ASTERISK TRIES TO EXPLAIN

I could be a star,
if that is what you want,
rising over the obscurity
of words, their bare limbs,

their lies that proclaim.
I could be just an eye
winking over the seriousness
of words, their dark intent,

their skeletons that rattle.
Or, I could be a burst of
petals over the heaviness
of words, higher than

their stones and dirt,
if that is what you want,
and avoid what crumbles.
It's all a matter of details

to further explain, what
you cannot see yet, with
this, my extra breath.
I could be a mote of dust,

if that is what you want,
just a speck, or a flake,
a raindrop, a nut, or a seed,
anything common or great.

It's all up to you now.
Try to imagine that I, the
asterisk, contain the world
in my one grain of sand.

TOP KILL FAILS

Top kill fails, but all
the other killing goes on,
wave after wave of oil
heading to the far shore.

It kills the sea turtles
and the seagulls and
even the sea grasses.
Nothing that swims in water

or lives near it will live.
It brings a toxic death
that spreads its brown
urge until it slides

into the dreams of fish
and turns them into
the dark light of nightmare.
So much killing is going

on that death has really
outdone itself this time,
wave after wave of oil
slapping the shore with

its reminder of pain.
All the water is dangerous
now for the fish and fowl.
All the warnings cannot

succeed in saving them,
as nothing can stop
wave after wave of oil,
the rhythm of this denial.

LEARNING THE HARD WAY

Life is hard, and the road
of life is quite hard, little
hard pebbles in the way
on the hard, packed dirt.

And it is hard to walk there
because usually the bright
sun makes it hard to see,
or the moonlight makes

it hard to see through
the shadows, and it is
hard to find a place to rest,
if the wind is blowing too

hard or if it is raining hard.
And it is hard to hear
the answer that makes
all this hard work worth it

when that question is asked.
It all seems like a hard
time and just another story
about hard luck and,

of course, hard feelings
that go along with this.
And then one develops
a hard heart, too, and

tough skin to endure it all.
And it is hard to find
a reason for going on, hard
to understand why it matters.

MORE ABOUT THE GRAVE DIGGERS

There's no magic in their
shovels that throw the dirt
over their shoulders onto
that ambitious pile,

though some difficult crumbs
keep on rolling back down.
Digging is a slow process.
But as they dig, they look

almost eternal when their
shovels glint in the sun
and when they keep time
with the tread in the clock.

And it all looks so well
planned, how to make more
room there in that earth
for yet another darkness,

as if that hole now waiting,
and square as a coffin,
knows what it must do
next when the burying begins.

Then the diggers go back
to finish what they started,
letting gravity take
the weight it wants to hold

and the death and stillness
it knows best how to keep.
Then their shovels know how
to pat that dirt down hard.

V

JUST PIECES IN A PUZZLE

What do they know now,
all these odd and dumb
shapes that lie unsolved
in a jumble on the table?

These pieces have no idea
how they will fit together,
or whether they ever
really will, or whether

one of them is missing,
and the whole picture
will never be complete.
So they lie there unsure

of their future now,
as they wait around for
the right hands that will
understand their ignorance,

and will know how
their colors and patterns
connect, so they can show
what they are a part of,

so that their meaning
gradually becomes clear,
the way a vague dream
might explain its confusion

and reasons, even to them.
So time is their friend
now until that brilliant
moment will finally shine.

A TEMPEST IN THE TEAPOT

It goes without saying
that this teapot with too
much wind and rain inside
will burst, even if that

storm is imagined and
the lightning is more like
a bad case of nerves and
the thunder is more like

a headache from too much
stress, but I'll say it now.
I'll also say that there
is no point in belittling

this teapot, just because
it is fragile and small,
and dainty, maybe with
little cut flowers painted

on its white china for trim.
It probably has a delicate
spout and handle, too, and
of course, an emotional lid,

which means that this teapot
is more than a metaphor,
as it sits there on the table
with a lace doily beneath it,

also a teacup and teaspoon
and a tea napkin nearby.
I'll say that no problem is
too small to brew up a storm.

NO ONE LIKES ROT

No one likes rot, its
slime and slow stink,
the garbage it is on
its way to decay and death,

its creeping disposition,
really an ill-humor,
and, most likely, never
in what most would call

a good mood or cheerful.
Rot has a hard time
being liked where it lives
in the dump or graveyard,

because it has been rejected.
And rot can't reverse
what it has become in
our eyes, the friend of

bacteria and foul fungus,
too much bad company
for us to tolerate its weak
character and morals.

Rot represents ruin and
all that can go wrong,
as it spoils all strength,
as it even helps out with

the putrefaction in hell.
So how else could we
speak of rot, but to condemn
it to rot in its place?

THESE ARE THE PITFALLS

Avoid the pitfalls of life,
the dangers you might
fall into, the broken bones
and bruises you might get,

not to mention the cuts
and wounds and the blood.
There is so much risk
wherever you walk, places

you might trip on, roots
you might stumble over,
the steps you might tumble
down, so that you fall hard.

Think about all the bumps
in the road just waiting
for you, the stones, bricks
and twigs, as if your path

were rigged for risk,
so your feet will find it.
Think about the potential
for harm that lies ahead

for you, even in the dusk
and the tricks in its shadows.
Loss is your specialty now,
and tears are the weather

that your emotions will
follow when you fall into
the deepest of those pitfalls
to meet your jagged pain.

THE GULF TURNS INTO TEARS

It isn't just the sadness
of the fish and birds
dying because the oil
has choked and killed them

that turns water into tears.
It isn't their dead bodies
washing up on the shores,
all dark and sticky,

and rigid, their eyes open,
as the tide of oil comes
in again, bathing them
with this accidental death.

Nor is it their last cries
that tried to reach out,
but instead were stifled
or swallowed up by the stench

of oil carried in the wind.
It's all of this together
that becomes the tragedy
of the oil, so that water

turns itself into tears,
salty and stinging and
swelling as it must endure
the pain that is endless.

And water turns itself into
tears, wave after wave, to
teach us how the oil and
the dead and sorrow add up.

SHOT IN THE FOOT

What's it like now to be
shot in the foot by yourself,
when you were aiming
elsewhere and didn't want

any kind of trouble?
How else could you frustrate
yourself more, what with
your foot oozing blood,

and the gun smoke clouding
the air so you can't think,
and that bird you wanted to
kill now flying away with

a flap that curiously sounds
like a laugh or like the
clapping after a clown show?
Why weren't you more careful

this time, since you now
can't walk far enough
to find help without leaving
another trail of blood, which

is the story of your life?
Who would help you anyway
to get that annoying bullet
out and to help you forget

the pain, when you didn't
happen to come here with anyone?
Isn't all this your fault
and this misery yours alone?

HEART IN THE RIGHT PLACE

So many sayings about
the HEART, the heavy HEART,
or a change of HEART,
or one has no HEART, or

to win one's HEART, or of
course, to break one's HEART.
I start to imagine that
it's a big job for the HEART

to mean so much during
the same time that it keeps
right on with the beating.
This includes at HEART

and by HEART and doing one's
HEART good and also from
the bottom of one's HEART,
as well as both to have

a HEART and have the HEART,
or to be near to one's HEART,
or to lose one's HEART,
such a sad matter there,

but then to set one's HEART
at rest and to one's content.
It really is all summed
up when I consider that I

take to HEART these sayings
with all of my HEART,
a rather HEARTFELT emotion
on my part, HEART-TO-HEART.

IF THE DEAD COULD DREAM

What would they dream
about besides the bones,
the loss, and the darkness?
What more would they

want besides all that,
and the sleep of eternity?
Would the dream be like
a complaint that something

was missing, not enough
air or space in the coffin?
Or too much time to dream?
Or too much time to think

about why they are dead?
Would the dead dream only
of their memories, since
they have no future?

Would the past let them
do that, repeat every voice
and gesture and action?
Or would the dead change

the past to comfort them,
no mistakes or regret?
How else could the dead
deal with what has happened

to them, shut as they are,
deep in the earth and away
from life and breath?
What else could they do?

HURRICANE GONE CRAZY

All my thoughts rush too
fast now like wind blasts
that make small seagulls
and sandpipers break their

wings so they cannot fly.
And then my loud roar, too,
makes rainwater hurt
itself as it bangs against

the rooftops and the waves
are forced to whip themselves,
tear and maul the sand
and hurt again the shore.

It's this spinning in my
words, too many clouds
speeding and out of control,
so that my breath can't catch

the logic that is right.
And now I must go on lashing
myself with all this hurt
and wrong so that every life

feels the pain that I feel.
Isn't that what going crazy
is all about, my untold
suffering that must hurl

itself onto the wide world,
in spite of the weather forecast,
and the severe damage from
my winds that violates me?

STAR WATCH

Beneath that mystery
of the sprinkle of light,
that sparkle and glint,
those jewels that decorate

the misunderstood darkness
of night, we must watch
to learn more about ourselves.
But what does the universe

know that we don't, so that
we must stare and understand?
Why must we ask the dim
constellations, so beautiful

and blind, to explain their
stories, as if they speak?
They're busy burning rock
out there, flame creating

its own purpose, gravity and
orbits defining attraction,
as light makes its argument
again against the night.

Still, we must watch
their dazzle and flickerings,
their bursts and settings,
their grim answers to our fate.

It's more work than what
mystery might expect from us,
our constant worship of
the mute and unexplained.

NAILED IN FOR GOOD

It is all over now, no more
to be seen of the hammer,
no more of that infernal
pounding that never seemed

to end, that drove you deep.
Now your position seems as
fixed as a star and your death
is the course you are set on,

surrounded as you are by
the silence of the dead wood
of this new coffin and by
the silence of this dead body.

You are buried together now
in this eternity of solitude
that you must share.
Here the darkness of death

suits you well as you can always
think about nothing now,
especially since the bones
don't ever bother you,

nor the ghost of the dead,
if there is one in this cemetery.
This is the place where
you have found peace and

the rest you need, where you,
as a nail, hold and are held.
This is the heaven for a nail,
where nothing ever weeps.

Printed in the USA
CPSIA information can be obtained
at www.ICGtesting.com
CBHW010022201024
16071CB00005B/25